W9-CPO-476

Rosh Hashanah

Buddy BOOKS
Holidays

ABDO
Publishing Company

A Buddy Book
by
Julie Murray

VISIT US AT
www.abdopublishing.com

Published by ABDO Publishing Company, PO Box 398166, Minneapolis, Minnesota 55439.

Printed in the United States of America, North Mankato, Minnesota.
092013
012014

 PRINTED ON RECYCLED PAPER

Coordinating Series Editor: Rochelle Baltzer
Editor: Sarah Tieck
Contributing Editors: Megan M. Gunderson, Marcia Zappa
Graphic Design: Denise Esner
Cover Photograph: *Getty Images*: Sally Moskol.
Interior Photographs/Illustrations: *AP Photo*: Diane Bondareff (p. 9), The Pantagraph, Lori Ann Cook-Neisler (p. 13), Press of Atlantic City, Dale Gerhard (p. 11), Chris Pizzello (p. 13); *Getty Images*: Paula Bronstein (p. 21); *Glow Images*: Godong (p. 6); *Shutterstock*: ChameleonsEye (p. 19), Margoe Edwards (p. 17), GWImages (p. 5), Aleksandar Todorovic (p. 15).

Library of Congress Cataloging-in-Publication Data

Murray, Julie, 1969- author.
  Rosh Hashanah / Julie Murray.
     p. cm. -- (Holidays)
  ISBN 978-1-62403-187-8
1. Rosh ha-Shanah--Juvenile literature. I. Title.
  BM695.N5M86 2013
  296.4'315--dc23
                         2013026940

Table of Contents

What Is Rosh Hashanah?

Rosh Hashanah is a Jewish holiday. It is often called the Jewish New Year. To honor it, people attend services and eat special foods. They think about the past year and the year to come.

Rosh Hashanah is usually in September or October. It can fall on any days of the week. Rosh Hashanah takes place on the first and second days of the Jewish month *Tishri*.

During Rosh Hashanah, synagogue services include the blowing of the shofar.

A Living Language

The Hebrew language has been around for thousands of years. *Rosh Hashanah* is Hebrew for "beginning of the year."

Today, millions of people in Israel speak Hebrew. This makes Hebrew one of the oldest living languages.

The oldest Jewish writings are in Hebrew.

The Story of Rosh Hashanah

Rosh Hashanah is also called the Day of Judgment and the Day of Remembrance. This holiday is described in the Bible.

Its name was first mentioned around the year 200. It was written in Jewish laws called the *Mishnah*.

Tishri is said to be the month God created the world. It marks the start of the Jewish year. So, Jews see Rosh Hashanah as a time of beginnings.

Rosh Hashanah begins a ten-day period called the Days of Awe. Jews believe that God judges all people during this time.

During Rosh Hashanah, Jews pray for God's forgiveness. They also pray for a good year and a long life.

The Days of Awe is a serious time. People pray and do good deeds. They do *Teshuvah*, or **repent**, and make up for their sins.

Traditions and Customs

During Rosh Hashanah, work is not allowed. People spend time at the **synagogue**. They read **holy** texts, sing, and pray.

Many people use a special greeting when they see each other. They say *"L'shanah tovah."* It means "for a good year" in Hebrew.

The bread tossed for Tashlikh stands for sins. When it washes away, it stands for people being cleansed.

Some Jews toss pieces of bread into flowing water. They say prayers as they do this. This is called *Tashlikh,* or "casting off."

The Shofar

The *shofar* is a ram's horn used as an instrument. It is part of Rosh Hashanah **synagogue** services.

The shofar blast is meant to call people to **repent**. It is blown after each of three special prayers. The shofar is used because it is mentioned in the Bible.

The person who blows the shofar is called the *tokea.*

Torah Time

During Rosh Hashanah, people avoid sleeping during the day. They spend time studying the Torah. And, they think about their **spiritual** life. They want to begin the year awake and ready.

The Torah is a group of holy writings. Some are kept on scrolls.

Rosh Hashanah Foods

People prepare certain foods for Rosh Hashanah. They often choose foods that are **symbols** of sweetness, blessings, and **abundance**. These are their hopes for the new year.

Round challah bread is served for Rosh Hashanah. The shape stands for the circle of life. Raisins may be baked in for more sweetness.

Bread and apples dipped in honey are Rosh Hashanah foods. Long ago, Jews believed apples helped people heal. Honey stands for sweetness. As they eat, they ask God to give them a sweet year.

During Rosh Hashanah, Jews may eat carrots or the head of a fish. These stand for success and happiness.

Pomegranates are another key food. They are said to have 613 seeds. These stand for the Torah's 613 *mitzvot*, or laws.

Pomegranates are mentioned many times in the Bible.

Rosh Hashanah Today

Rosh Hashanah is considered one of the most important Jewish holidays. Even people who are not Jewish may honor the holiday. They reflect on their lives. Rosh Hashanah is a time for new beginnings.

Some Jews cover their heads while praying.

Yom Kippur

Yom Kippur (yohm-kih-PUR) happens shortly after Rosh Hashanah. It is the last day of the Days of Awe. It is also known as the Day of **Atonement**.

On Yom Kippur, Jews attend **synagogue** services. They do not work or eat. They think about their sins and ask for forgiveness.

Important Words

abundance a large amount of something.

atonement doing acts such as fasting or praying as ways to make up for sins.

holy important to a religion.

repent to feel bad about one's sins, ask for forgiveness, and decide to do what is right.

spiritual (SPIHR-ih-chuh-wuhl) of or relating to the spirit or soul instead of physical things.

symbol (SIHM-buhl) an object or mark that stands for an idea.

synagogue (SIH-nuh-gahg) a special place where Jewish people gather to pray.

Web Sites

To learn more about Rosh Hashanah, visit ABDO Publishing Company online. Web sites about Rosh Hashanah are featured on our Book Links page. These links are routinely monitored and updated to provide the most current information available.

www.abdopublishing.com

Index